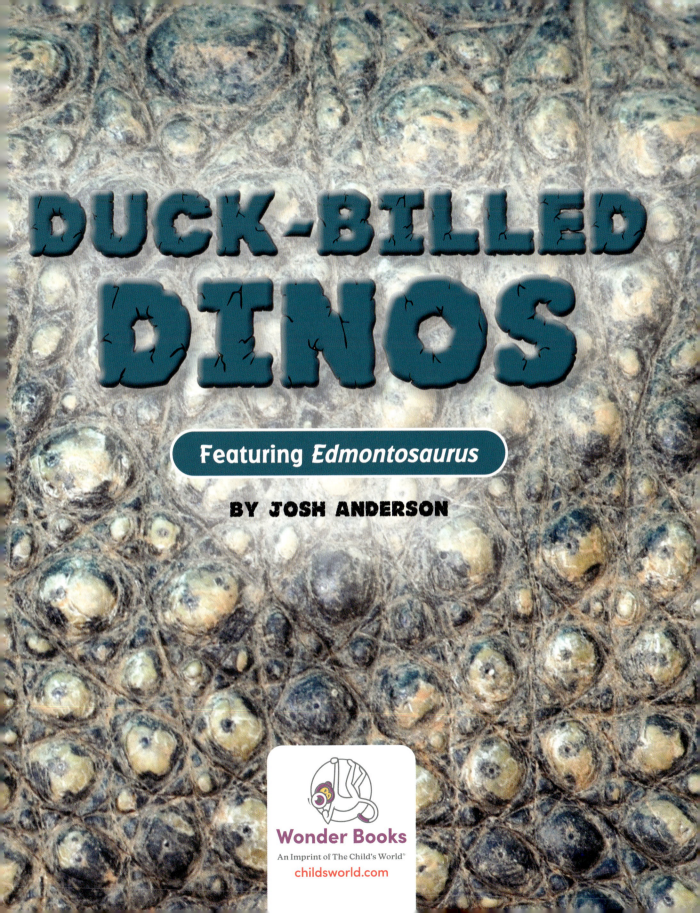

DUCK-BILLED DINOS

Featuring *Edmontosaurus*

BY JOSH ANDERSON

Wonder Books
An Imprint of The Child's World®
childsworld.com

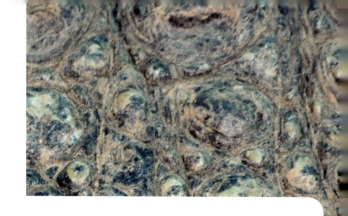

Published by The Child's World®
800-599-READ • www.childsworld.com

Copyright © 2023 by The Child's World®
All rights reserved. No part of this book may be reproduced or utilized in any form or by any means without written permission from the publisher.

Photography Credits
Cover: ©Warpaintcobra; page 1: ©Pan Xunbin / Shutterstock; page 5: ©Roman Garcia Mora/Stocktrek Images / Getty Images; page 6: ©FunkMonk / Wikimedia; page 9: ©FunkMonk / Wikimedia; page 10: ©Kurt Miller/Stocktrek Images / Getty Images; page 11: ©Warpaint / Shutterstock; page 13: ©fcdb / Getty Images; page 14: ©Warpaintcobra / Getty Images; page 15: ©Jim Channell / Getty Images; page 16: ©Tuul & Bruno Morandi / Getty Images; page 16: ©Julio Francisco; page 17: ©Julio Francisco; page 19: ©picture alliance / Contributor / Getty Images; page 21: ©CookiesForDevo / Getty Images

ISBN Information
9781503865228 (Reinforced Library Binding)
9781503865846 (Portable Document Format)
9781503866683 (Online Multi-user eBook)
9781503867529 (Electronic Publication)

LCCN 2022940910

Printed in the United States of America

About the Author

Josh Anderson has published more than 50 books for children and young adults. His two sons, Leo and Dane, are the greatest joys in his life. Josh's hobbies include coaching youth basketball, no-holds-barred games of Exploding Kittens, reading, and family movie nights. His favorite dinosaur is a secret he'll never share!

CONTENTS

Digging for Bones...4

What We Know...11

Keep Searching...18

Glossary...22
Wonder More...23
Learn More...24
Index...24

CHAPTER 1

Digging for Bones

Pretend you can time travel to a prehistoric age.... You've gone back about 66 million years. You're in a forest in North America. In the distance, you hear a roar. You know that *Tyrannosaurus rex* (teh-ran-uh-SAWR-uss REKS), or *T. rex*, lived at this time and place. It's a good bet that the **apex predator** is looking for its next meal. A huge creature runs through the trees. You think it must be *T. rex*. But this giant doesn't look as fierce as a *T. rex*. Its face is long and shaped like a duck's bill. It chews a pine cone with its strong teeth. This must be *Edmontosaurus* (ed-mon-toh-SAWR-uss), one of the duck-billed dinosaurs . . . and a frequent meal for a hungry *T. rex*.

How do we know so much about creatures who lived long before the first humans? The simple answer: SCIENCE! Let's learn more!

Edmontosaurus was as big as a fire truck!

Edmontosaurus is one of North America's most commonly studied dinosaurs.

Humans have been studying *Edmontosaurus* for more than 130 years. For years, *Edmontosaurus* was called by a few other names. It was named *Edmontosaurus* in 1917. The name comes from the city of Edmonton in Canada. *Edmontosaurus* was not found in Edmonton. But it was found nearby. There has been a lot of debate over which dinosaurs should be called *Edmontosaurus*.

An *Edmontosaurus* skeleton was one of the first dinosaurs ever displayed in the United States that was made up of real **fossils**. It was first shown to the public in 1901. You can still see it today at the Yale Peabody Museum in New Haven, Connecticut.

One of the most fascinating dinosaur finds ever was the *Edmontosaurus* mummy. A mummy is a body that has been **preserved**, either in special wrappings or by certain conditions in nature.

The mummy fossil was discovered in the United States in 1908. It may have dried out before its soft parts could rot away. Then, it got buried in sand or mud. Because it was so well-preserved, there was an imprint of *Edmontosaurus's* skin on the bones. This has helped scientists understand what its skin texture may have been like. **CT scans** and X-rays might even help the scientists see impressions of the dinosaur's organs

The *Edmontosaurus* mummy is still on display at the American Museum of Natural History in New York City.

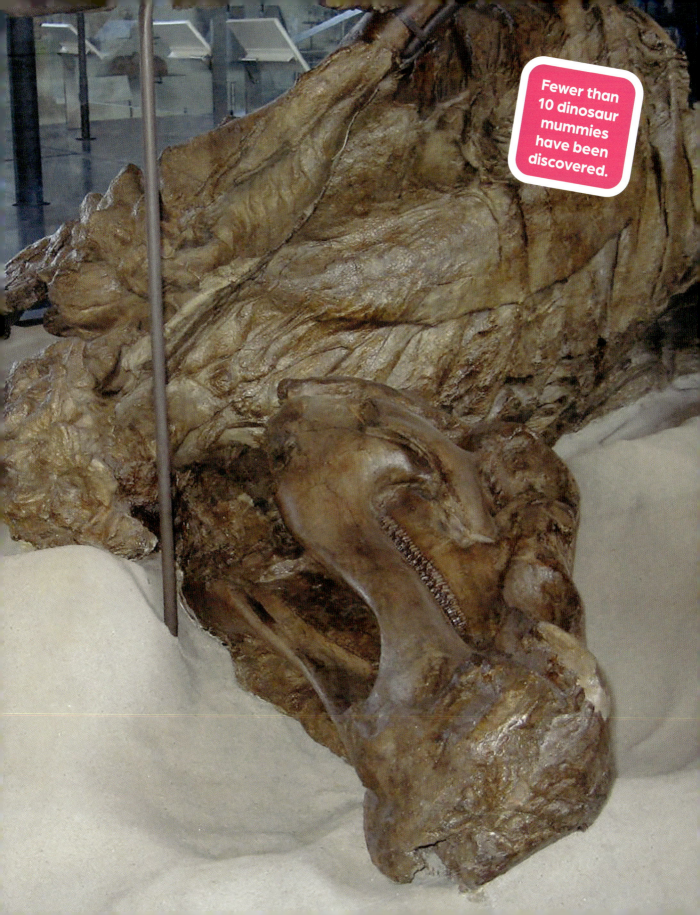

Fewer than 10 dinosaur mummies have been discovered.

While no one is sure of *Edmontosaurus's* exact color, the dino is often drawn with stripes and a colored bill.

CHAPTER 2

What We Know

Edmontosaurus belongs to a group of dinosaurs called hadrosaurs. Hadrosaurs all had long, flat snouts. They also had hundreds of teeth. Hadrosaurs are divided into two groups. Some had hard bumps called crests on their heads. These may have been used to make noise. Other hadrosaurs, like *Edmontosaurus*, either had no crests or had smaller, soft skin crests.

When It Lived: 66 million years ago –
The Late Cretaceous Period
Where It Lived: North America; forests
First Discovered: 1892

Edmontosaurus was a herbivore. That means it ate plants. It used its wide snout to grab plants and leaves. *Edmontosaurus* had hundreds of teeth. It walked on four feet, but it could also run on two feet.

FUN FACTS

- Some scientists thought *Edmontosaurus* lived in the water. But this has proven to be false.
- Its name means "Edmonton lizard." Its bones were found in Alberta, a province in Canada. Edmonton is the capital of Alberta.
- Tanzania, a country in Africa, put *Edmontosaurus* on a postage stamp in 1991.
- One *Edmontosaurus* skeleton shows evidence that it survived an attack by a **theropod**. But the *Edmontosaurus* may have died later from an infection caused by the attack.
- *Edmontosaurus* had over 1,000 teeth.

THEN AND NOW

In addition to thinking it lived in the water, some **paleontologists** thought *Edmontosaurus* ate like a duck! A research paper from 1970 describes how one scientist thought *Edmontosaurus* used its duckbill. The scientist wrote that *Edmontosaurus* used its bill to filter out water as it ate. Now scientists believe *Edmontosaurus* usually ate on dry land.

Tanzania was home to many dinosaurs, including *Edmontosaurus*. The country honored its history with several dino postage stamps.

Lambeosaurus had a crest on its head that resembled a hatchet.

Edmontosaurus wasn't the only duck-billed dinosaur. Here are a couple of others from the ancient world.

Lambeosaurus (lam-bee-oh-SAWR-uss) had a huge, unique crest on its head. It lived in North America at the same time as Edmontosaurus.

Maiasaura (my-uh-SAWR-uh) means "good mother lizard." It was named this because it's the first dinosaur ever discovered next to its eggs and babies. It also lived in North America at the same time as Edmontosaurus.

UP FOR DEBATE

We now know that hadrosaurs like Edmontosaurus lived and ate on land. Some scientists are even questioning their duck-billed nature. The surface of animals' bills and beaks are made of keratin. Keratin dissolves quickly. So scientists aren't sure what shape an ancient bill might've had. Some scientists think Edmontosaurus's "duckbill" may have been more like a "shovel beak."

EDMONTOSAURUS
(ed-mon-toh-SAWR-uss) VS

Length: 42 feet (13 m)

Weight: 7,500 pounds (3,402 kilograms)

Top Speed: 28 miles (45 kilometers) per hour

Weakness: Size; no way to fight off predators

Best Weapon or Defense: Good eyesight, hearing, and sense of smell may have helped avoid predators

PARASAUROLOPHUS
(payr-uh-sawr-AWL-uh-fus)

Length: 36 feet (11 m)

Weight: 5,600 pounds (2,540 kg)

Top Speed: 25 miles (40 km) per hour

Weakness: Size

Best Weapon or Defense: Six-foot-long crest on its head helped to make loud sounds which may have scared off predators

CHAPTER 3

Keep Searching

Scientists learn most of what they know about dinosaurs from just a few fossils. Every discovery can teach us something new. Modern technology can help. New tools help us learn more about old bones.

Most scientists did not think *Edmontosaurus* had a crest on top of its head. But a recent discovery may show otherwise. An *Edmontosaurus* **specimen** was found with traces of a small crest on its skull. Using a medical scanner, scientists were able to tell that the crest was soft. It may have been similar to a rooster's comb.

As new technology becomes available, scientists can learn more about ancient dinosaur bones.

Edmontosaurus „Schnabel-Dinosaurier"
Edmontosaurus annectens (Marsh 1892) "Duckbilled dinosaur"

Sometimes a second look at a fossil may lead to a new scientific discovery. In 2020, scientists examined some bones. The bones were found in northern Alaska's Arctic region. Scientists thought the bones belonged to a smaller relative of *Edmontosaurus*. Another look at the bones showed otherwise. They were actually from a young *Edmontosaurus*. Its bones had never been found that far north before. The discovery changed scientists' understanding of how and where this giant of the past lived.

Who will make the next important dinosaur discovery? It might just be YOU!

Edmontosaurus had around 1,000 teeth, arranged in rows, with more replacement teeth under each row.

GLOSSARY

apex predator (AY-pecks PREH-duh-tur): an animal that hunts other animals but is not hunted itself

CT Scan (C T SKAN): a more powerful kind of X-ray that shows better detail

fossil (FAH-sul): the remains or traces of plants and animals that lived long ago

paleontologists (pay-lee-on-TOL-uh-jists): scientists who study plants and animals that lived millions of years ago

prehistoric (pree-hiss-TORE-ick): belonging to a period in a time before written history

preserved (pruh-ZERVED): protected from harm for future use

specimen (SPEH-seh-mehn): a material used in testing, examination, or study

theropod (THEYR-uh-pod): a carnivorous dinosaur that walked on its back two legs

WONDER MORE

Think About It: How would your life be different if your head were shaped differently? Imagine it is long and somewhat flat, like *Edmontosaurus*. What activities would be harder to do? Would there be any advantages?

Talk About It: Many of the hadrosaurs had crests on their heads. They came in different shapes and sizes. Ask your friends and family what kind of crest they'd prefer if they were a dinosaur. Would they want something small, like the one *Edmontosaurus* may have had? Or would they prefer a huge crest, like *Parasaurolophus*?

Write About It: Imagine a world long after humans no longer exist. Write a story from the perspective of an alien studying Earth and trying to figure out what humans were like.

MESOZOIC ERA

Triassic Period	Jurassic Period	Cretaceous Period
201–252 Million Years Ago	145–201 Million Years Ago	66–145 Million Years Ago

LEARN MORE

BOOKS

Kelly, Erin Suzanne. *Dinosaurs*. New York: Children's Press, 2021.

Pimentel, Annette Bay, and Daniele Fabbri. *Do You Really Want to Meet Edmontosaurus?* Mankato, MN: Amicus, 2020.

Weakland, Mark. *Duck-billed Dinosaurs: Ranking Their Speed, Strength, and Smarts*. Mankato, MN: Black Rabbit Books, 2020.

WEBSITES

Visit our website for links about *Edmontosaurus*: **childsworld.com/links**

Note to Parents, Caregivers, Teachers, and Librarians: We routinely verify our web links to make sure they are safe and active sites. So encourage your readers to check them out!

INDEX

Alaska, 20
Alberta, 12
American Museum of Natural History, 8
Arctic, 20

bones, 8, 12, 18–20

Canada, 7, 12
crests, 11
Cretaceous Period, 11

Edmonton, 7, 12

hadrosaurs, 11, 15

Lambeosaurus, 14–15

Maiasaura, 15
mummy, 8

New Haven, Connecticut, 7
New York City, 8

North America, 4, 6, 11, 15

teeth, 4, 11–12, 21
Tyrannosaurus rex, 4

United States, 7–8

Yale Peabody Museum, 7